Missed
and
Txt Me

Jillian Powell

Illustrated by
Paul Savage

Titles in Full Flight 3

Web Cam Scam	Jillian Powell
Nervous	Tony Norman
Splitzaroni	Kathryn White
Missed Call	Jillian Powell
Space Pirates	David Orme
Basketball War	Jonny Zucker
Survival	Chris Buckton
Killer Sharks	Stan Cullimore
Sprinters	Jonny Zucker
Dangerous Stunts	Jonny Zucker

Badger Publishing Limited
26 Wedgwood Way, Pin Green Industrial Estate,
Stevenage, Hertfordshire SG1 4QF
Telephone: 01438 356907. Fax: 01438 747015.
www.badger-publishing.co.uk
enquiries@badger-publishing.co.uk

Missed Call   ISBN 978 1 84424 236 8

Text © Jillian Powell 2004
Series editing © Jonny Zucker 2004
Complete work © Badger Publishing Limited 2004

All rights reserved. No part of this publication may be reproduced, stored in any form or by any means mechanical, electronic, recording or otherwise without the prior permission of the publisher.

The right of Jillian Powell to be identified as author of this Work has been asserted by her in accordance with the Copyright, Designs and Patents Act 1988.

Series Editor: Jonny Zucker
Publisher: David Jamieson
Editor: Paul Martin
Design: Jain Birchenough
Cover illustration: Paul Savage

Missed Call

Contents

Chapter 1	Scrambled Brains	4
Chapter 2	The Fun Run	7
Chapter 3	Missed Call	9
Chapter 4	Switched Off	11
Chapter 5	More Missed Calls	13
Chapter 6	Trapped	16

Txt Me

Contents

Chapter 1	Monster Phone	20
Chapter 2	Playground Nightmare	22
Chapter 3	New Boy	25
Chapter 4	A Text Message	27
Chapter 5	Result!	29
Chapter 6	M8s	31

Badger Publishing

Chapter 1 - Scrambled Brains

"Hi Pete."

"Hi Danny."

"Look mate, check these out!"
Danny put his feet up on the bed and pointed the mobile at his trainers.
"Cool or what?"

"They look great, Danny," Pete said.

"Danny!" Mum appeared at the door. "You're not on that thing again!" she said. "I sometimes wonder if it's fixed to your head. You'll scramble your brains, you know. Who are you talking to?"

"Just Pete."

"Pete lives next door, for heavens sake," Mum said. "Have you thought of talking face to face?"

"What's going on?" Pete asked Danny.

"It's just Mum," Danny said. "She says I'm scrambling my brains."

"Your brains are scrambled already mate," Pete said.

"You coming on that fun run on Sunday?" Danny asked Pete.

"No Dan, I've downloaded this new game," Pete told Danny. "It's really cool. It's a sea rescue… these guys are all jumping out of this plane and…"

It sounded great. But Danny was still looking forward to the fun run.

Chapter 2 - The Fun Run

It was the day of the fun run. It had been raining all night and the ground was very wet. The runners splashed through giant puddles and across fields that felt like sponges under foot.

Towards the end, it began to rain again. Danny arrived home wet and covered in mud. He was panting for breath and his knees were red from the cold and the rain.

"That lot will have to go into the washing machine right away," Mum said. "And look at those new trainers!"

Danny rang Pete. He wanted to tell him about the fun run and show him the state of his trainers. This picture messaging was great. Danny dialled Pete's number.

The mobile phone you are calling is switched off. Please try later.

Chapter 3 - Missed Call

Danny tried ringing Pete a couple of times but his phone was still switched off. Pete wasn't in school the next day either.

Danny had his martial arts class after school. He had tried to get Pete to come along to classes but Pete said he didn't fancy being thrown around on a mat by some power-crazed loony dressed in pyjamas.

When Danny got home, mum was preparing tea.

"That thing has been bleeping," she told Danny, nodding to his mobile.

Missed call.

Danny dialled his messages.

You have one new message.

"Danny, it's Pete. Where are you mate? I need you to call me. I mean call me now. When you get in. I think I'm in trouble, Dan. Just call me, right?"

Chapter 4 - Switched Off

Danny dialled Pete's number.

Calling. The mobile phone you are calling is switched off. Please try later.

"Great!" Danny thought. "He asks me to call right away, then he switches his phone off."

Danny had to go to football practice. Pete had stopped going lately. He said he didn't see the point in getting cold and wet and having Tin-head Thomson shout at you when you could be at home playing some cool new game.

"Pete, mate. Look, you said to call. I'm calling, right? And now you've switched your phone off. What's the deal? Look, give me a call back."

Danny kept his phone on, risking Tin-head's fury. But it didn't ring. He kept thinking about Pete's call all through football practice. Pete's voice had sounded funny. He sounded as if he was in real trouble. Danny made up his mind to ring again after the match.

Chapter 5 - More Missed Calls

Missed Call.

So Danny's phone had rung after all. With the noise of the match, and Thomson shouting his head off, Danny hadn't heard it. He quickly dialled up his messages.

You have three new messages.

Message one.

Danny's heart began to beat faster.

"Danny mate, it's Pete. Look, you've got to help me, mate. I'm in trouble here."

Message two.

"I think I'm trapped, Danny.
You have to help me."

Message three.

"Danny, it's hell in here.
You have to get me out."

Danny's fingers were shaking as he dialled Pete's number.

This time Pete answered. He had turned on picture messaging. His face looked white and his voice had a strange echo.

"Danny, is that you?"

"Yes, Pete, it's me. Where are you?"

"I'm trapped, mate. I'm in this locker."

"Locker? What sort of locker?"

"At school. In the lockers at school."

Danny was silent for a moment. This must be a wind-up. But Pete's face was deadly serious.

"Just get here, Danny. Come and get me out. I can't get out, mate."

There was real panic in Pete's voice. "Okay, Pete. I'm on my way."

Chapter 6 - Trapped

The school was closed but Mr Marsh the caretaker was still there.

"Mr Marsh, I've left something in my locker," Danny said.

"Can't it wait till the morning?" Mr Marsh said.

"I really need it tonight... for homework," Danny lied.

"All right. But don't be too long. I was just on my way home," Mr Marsh told him.

Danny headed straight for the locker room.

It was in the basement. The tall lockers filled one whole side of the room. They were steely grey, each one with a key and padlock.

"Pete! It's me, Danny. Where are you? Look, shout or knock or something."

Danny felt stupid. He was talking to the wall.

He took out his mobile and rang Pete's number.

Calling.

There was Pete's white face again. "Get me out mate, please. Just get me out."

"Where are you, which locker?" Danny asked.

"My locker, in my locker."

Pete's locker was next to Danny's own. It was locked and there was no key. He would have to force it open.

He used his penknife and a steel ruler. At last the door burst open. The locker was empty… except for Pete's phone.

"Okay mate, joke over," Danny said.

"You don't understand mate," Pete said. "I said I'm trapped. I'm trapped in this phone."

Danny flipped open the phone. Pete's white face stared out at him. Pete was just a face, a picture message, trapped in a mobile phone…

* * *

Txt Me!

Chapter 1 - Monster Phone

"But mum..."

"No buts," Mum said. "It is very good of Nan to let you have her old phone."

"But it's so big and ugly." Kirsty said. She looked at the phone with disgust. It was massive and black. It weighed a ton. She couldn't take that thing to school. It would be a joke.

"A phone is a phone," Mum said. "It's for emergencies."

A phone is a phone. How wrong could anyone be? Gemma Roberts' phone was space age. It had a colour screen and multi-media messaging. She could get the football scores on it, and even get a shot of the winning goal. It made Nan's old phone look like something that went out with the dinosaurs.

"I can't take that thing to school," Kirsty moaned. "You don't know what it's like, Mum."

"Put it in your bag," Mum said. "I'll ring you later, to check if it's working."

Kirsty looked at the phone. Perhaps if she could get a friendly steamroller to run over it...

Chapter 2 -
Playground Nightmare

"You connected yet, Kirsty?"

It was Gemma Roberts, the playground bully at Kirsty's new school. Kirsty hated her new school. She hated Gemma Roberts even more.

"I... yeah. I've got a phone, if I need it."

Gemma stared at her. Some of her mates were gathering round.

"Let's see then."

"No. I mean, it's at the bottom of my bag..."

Then something awful happened.

Kirsty's phone began to ring.

Kirsty ran across the playground. She fumbled in her bag and took out the phone.

It was Mum.

"Just to say I will be a bit late home tonight," she said. "The key is in the usual place."

"Okay Mum, see you."

Kirsty turned the thing off. But it was too late. Gemma Roberts had seen it. She started to laugh.

"Check this out, you lot!"

Gemma grabbed the phone.

She pretended to drop it, because it was so heavy. Then she threw it to one of her mates.

The phone crashed to the floor.

Kirsty went to pick it up. To her horror, it wasn't broken...

Chapter 3 - New Boy

The next day, the headmaster appeared in Kirsty's class before Assembly. He had a new boy with him.

"This is Simon," Mr Weeks announced. "He is joining us today, and I am sure you will all make him very welcome."

Simon sat down in the front row of the class. He wore thick glasses and looked terrified.

"Hey, Speccy four-eyes. Is that board close enough for you?"

It was Gemma Roberts.

Simon didn't turn round. Gemma began to flick balls of paper at him. "Hey, four-eyes!"

Still Simon didn't turn round. Kirsty felt sorry for him. She scribbled a note that said 'Gemma Roberts is an idiot. Take no notice', and added her name and mobile number. She passed it to Simon.

Simon read it and turned round with a grateful smile. Poor Simon, Kirsty thought. But there was one good thing. Perhaps now Gemma would forget about her Nan's phone.

Chapter 4 - A Text Message

No such luck. Gemma was having fun.

"I hear the museum is looking for old relics," she told Kirsty. "They'd love your phone."

Kirsty began to walk away. But Gemma grabbed her bag again. She took out Kirsty's phone and began to stagger under its weight. Then she looked at the screen.

"Hey, Kirsty. You've got a text! I think it's from... a dinosaur!"

The others fell about laughing. Kirsty grabbed the phone back. The amazing thing was, she did have a message.

It said simply: | TXT ME |

Kirsty frowned. Who could be texting her?

She punched out a reply.

| WHO R U? | | A M8 |

"Who is it, Kirsty?" Gemma asked.

"It's a mate," Kirsty said, turning her back on Gemma.

At least they had stopped laughing. They seemed a bit surprised she had a text. But not as surprised as Kirsty was.

Chapter 5 - Result!

Gemma was standing in the middle of a crowd.

"I'll get the score any minute now," she promised the others. "We'll soon see how the match is going."

Then Kirsty's phone bleeped. She had got used to it now. The texts seemed to come whenever she was in trouble, or needed help. This time she stared in amazement. Then she read aloud:

```
"REAL 1 MAN U 2"
```

The Man U supporters began to shout and clap, except for Gemma Roberts who looked furious.

She was blinking at the screen on her phone. Then the score flashed through. But it was too late. Kirsty's old phone had beaten her.

Then one of her gang called out, "Check out the chart, Gemma. I want to know if that track made number one."

Right on cue, Kirsty's phone bleeped. "Yeah, it has," she said casually.

Gemma was still staring at her phone. Kirsty had beaten her yet again.

But where were these texts coming from? It seemed like they were magic.

She sent a text back.

```
M8S.  4EVR.  AGN D RST.
```

Chapter 6 - M8s

Gemma soon lost interest in Kirsty's phone. After all, people now asked Kirsty the latest updates. But she still made Simon's life a misery.

Kirsty found Simon sitting alone in the the playground. She went and stood behind the seat. "You okay, mate?"

"I hate them," Simon cried. "Look what they've done." Simon's glasses were lying on the ground, smashed.

Then Kirsty heard a bleeping sound. "Hey, look. You've got a text."

"But I can't see a thing," Simon said.

"Do you want me to read it?" Kirsty asked. "It might be important."

Kirsty peered at the screen. She read the message. But she didn't need to. It was her reply to her mysterious text friend.

"It was you sending me all those texts, wasn't it?" Kirsty said slowly.

"Look, I may be the new boy and have glasses, but I've got the works on this thing." Simon told her. "Between us, we can beat that Roberts any day!"

"That's it then," Kirsty said, sitting down beside him. "Mates? Forever? Against the rest?"

Simon peered at his phone and punched out:

```
M8S.  4EVR.  AGN D RST.
```